INSIDER'S GUIDE TO
CHINA DOLL COLLECTING

by Jan Foulke

Photographs by **Howard Foulke**

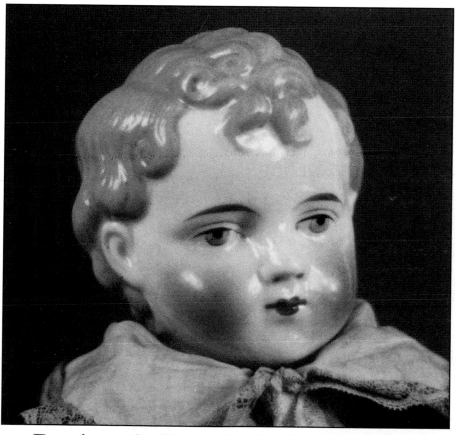

Buying, Selling & Collecting Tips

Published by **Hobby House Press**
Hobby
Grantsvi

Other Titles by Author:

Blue Book of Dolls & Values®
2nd Blue Book of Dolls & Values®
3rd Blue Book of Dolls & Values®
4th Blue Book of Dolls & Values®
5th Blue Book of Dolls & Values®
6th Blue Book of Dolls & Values®
7th Blue Book of Dolls & Values®
8th Blue Book of Dolls & Values®
9th Blue Book of Dolls & Values®
10th Blue Book of Dolls & Values®
11th Blue Book of Dolls & Values®
12th Blue Book of Dolls & Values®

Focusing on Effanbee Composition Dolls
Focusing on Treasury of
Mme. Alexander Dolls
Focusing on Gebrüder Heubach Dolls
Kestner: King of Dollmakers
Simon & Halbig Dolls: The Artful Aspect
Doll Classics
Focusing on Dolls
Buying & Selling Dolls
German "Dolly" Collecting

The registered trademarks, the trademarks and the copyrights appearing in this book belong to the company under whose name they appear, unless otherwise noted.

The doll prices noted within this book are intended as value guides rather than arbitrarily set prices. Retail prices in this book are recorded as accurately as possible but in the case of errors, typographical, clerical or otherwise, the author and publisher assume no liability nor responsibility for any loss incurred by users of this book.

COVER: 13-1/2in (34cm) 1850s china with so-called covered wagon hairdo. *H & J Foulke, Inc.*

TITLE PAGE: This very nice boy with two curls falling onto his forehead appears to be from the Alt, Beck & Gottschalck factory, although he has no mark. His hair is very well modeled with molded comb marks and curls. His ears are exposed. *H & J Foulke, Inc.*

BACK COVER: This pretty 16in (42cm) lady has light brown hair, called *café-au-lait* by collectors, in the style known as "curly top." This head is also found with black hair. *H & J Foulke, Inc.*

ADDITIONAL COPIES AVAILABLE @ $9.95 plus postage
FROM
HOBBY HOUSE PRESS, INC.
ONE CORPORATE DRIVE
GRANTSVILLE, MD 21536
1-800-554-1447

© 1995 by Jan and Howard Foulke

Printed in the United States of America

ISBN: 0-87588-441-5

TABLE OF CONTENTS

Questions from Collectors – Answers from an Insider

A one-of-a-kind?

Curly "do."

Rare doll.

TABLE OF CONTENTS
Questions from Collectors – Answers from an Insider

KPM original.

The beginning...

Unusual features.

INTRODUCTION

China head dolls are simply amazing when one considers their longevity. They were made as children's playthings for nearly 100 years in basically the same form with just some stylistic changes. Wood, cloth, and papier-mâché were also constant materials, but they went through many metamorphoses, whereas chinas changed very little except for updating the hairstyles.

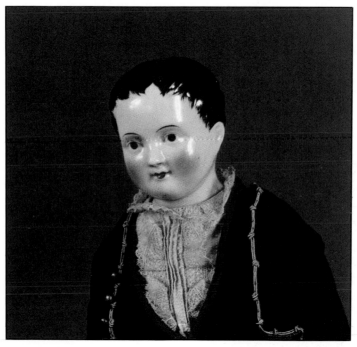

A very good example of a 20in (51cm) boy of the 1850s with windblown hair and brush marks around his face, desirable large brown eyes and nice and appropriate old clothing, which appears to be original. It seems that dolls dressed as boys or men were not much played with because many of them still survive in their original clothing. *Private Collection.*

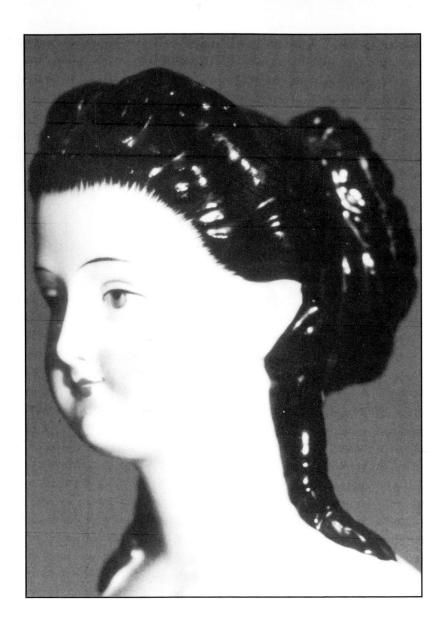

A lovely black-haired lady of the 1870s with hair brush-stroked away from the face into first a roll, then a cluster of loose curls and a long curl flowing onto the shoulders from behind each ear. She has lovely blue eyes and has almost a smiling expression. *Private Collection.*

Back in the 1930s and 1940s when doll collecting was just getting started, china head dolls were very popular with collectors. Bisque dolls were considered nearly new in those days, for many of the collectors had played with bisque dolls themselves and bought bisque dolls for their children. But even then china dolls were old, and some of them were nearly 100 years old. Actually, so little was known about china dolls then, that most collectors didn't even know which ones were the oldest. They called china heads "Staffordshire" or "Chelsea" after English pottery towns, not knowing the heads were actually German in origin. However, with the doll research available to collectors today, we now have a lot more information to study about china head dolls. We have even begun to identify some of the manufacturers. But there are still many unanswered questions about china head dolls. Perhaps you, as a collector, will discover some new information from studying the dolls that you collect.

Sometime during the 1960s, china dolls fell from favor, and bisque dolls became the big collecting rage in the doll world – with a sharp escalation in prices of bisque dolls accompanying this phenomenon. In contrast, china dolls have remained quiet but have shown a slow, steady increase in value. So far, they have escaped the up and down prices of the French and cloth doll markets.

When I first became interested in dolls 22 years ago, I was an antiques dealer, not really a doll collector. I was advised not to buy china head dolls because they would not sell. I was told nobody wants them. But I thought that they were charming and interesting. Also, it seemed to me they were a good value, considering that they were true antiques. So I did buy them, and I always sold them – every one I ever bought. I never got stuck with any that didn't sell. Sometimes I have in my business inventory a bisque doll, or cloth doll, or composition doll that I just can't sell. It seems as if, for no really good reason, no one else wants the doll, but I have never had that happen with a china head doll!

I always advise collectors to buy what they like. Don't let someone else tell you what you should buy. Your collection is your hobby and should be based upon your enjoyment of it. Your collection should reflect your own tastes and interests, not those of some arbitrary group that says this is good to collect or that is bad to collect. If you like and enjoy china dolls, then by all means collect them.

Today there is in doll collecting a group of dedicated china head collectors, but they are far outnumbered by the bisque doll lovers. However, the time seems right as we come to the end of the 20th century for a resurgence of interest in china head dolls. Indeed, I think the resurgence may be starting, if we can judge by the number of people who ask for information about china head dolls.

For those interested in collecting china head dolls, for those who just want to look at pictures of china head dolls and for those who have found an old china head doll in the attic or at an estate sale and want to know more about it, we have written this book. Of course, in a book of this size, we cannot provide an exhaustive study of every aspect of this special field of doll collecting, but we will present an overview of more than 100 years of china dolls.

WHAT IS A CHINA DOLL?

Actually, china head dolls are made of the same materials as the fine china dishes that you, your mother, or grandmother puts on the dining room table for special dinners. The term *china* comes from the country of China, where the formula for

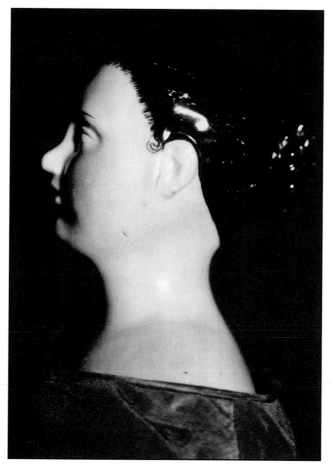

This 19in (48cm) china head lady of the 1840s has a great profile. She also has tiny brush strokes indicating her hairline, with hair pulled back into a heavy, braided bun; particularly notice the terrific little curl above her ear and her molded upper eyelid. She is an outstanding example of an early china head doll and brought $6600 at auction in June 1993. *Frances Walker Collection. Courtesy of Richard W. Withington, Inc.*

porcelain was an old secret for 1,000 years before it was made in Germany. China is a glazed porcelain, which is made from a carefully composed mixture of kaolin or china clay, fine sand and two minerals: feldspar and quartz. Early manufacturers made a paste of this mix and rolled it out like dough, then pressed it into molds. Later methods used a more liquid slip that could be poured into molds. (If you look inside a china head you can tell whether it was pressed or poured. If it was pressed, the inside will be rough and the thickness uneven. If it was poured, the inside will be smooth and of a uniform thickness.) When the pieces are set, the molds are removed and the heads are fired at a very high temperature in a large kiln or oven until they become hard. After they cool, they are sanded until they are very smooth. Then they are painted, first with a complexion tint, if used, then the hair and features. After the paint has dried, the glaze is applied, sometimes by dipping the head in the liquid glaze mixture, which is made of the same ingredients as the slip but in different proportions. The head is then fired again to set the colors and the glaze, but this time at a low temperature.

China dolls typically have only their head and shoulders, and sometimes their lower limbs, made of china. But there are exceptions, as you will see in this book, including the fragile all-china dolls or Frozen Charlottes. The china head and shoulder piece is simply referred to as a shoulder head. This head is usually put on a cloth body, sometimes with leather hands or with china lower arms and legs. The china foot has painted and molded boots, white china stockings, and a painted garter, usually blue, tied below the knee. Boots made before 1870 have flat soles; after that date, the boots were made with heels. Some of the molded and painted boots are very intricate and beautifully modeled with details of gussets, piping, tassels and buttons. Colors, in addition to the common black, include light and dark blue, orange, light and dark green, pink, and gray. Some boots are very fancy and feature two colors, such as gray and dark blue. Garters of blue, pink, green or lavender were painted just below the knee to give extra color, detail and interest to the lower leg.

Sometimes a kid or leather body was used for a china head doll. You will find all sorts of variations in head and body combinations with china head dolls because the porcelain factories that made the heads and limbs were seldom the factories that put the dolls together. This was generally done by a toy or doll factory that ordered the china parts from a porcelain factory, then added bodies to complete the dolls. Many china heads, arms and legs were sold directly to the retail trade through stores and catalogs. Bodies were made for these dolls at home. Many women's magazines published patterns for making doll bodies as well as doll clothes. Some seamstresses designed their own doll bodies. Some of these bodies are quite clumsy and out of proportion. They are what I call "clunkers." However, if they are original to the head, they should be preserved as a matter of historical importance even if they are not very attractive. "Doing up dolls" was a popular activity in those old days when women did not usually work outside the home.

A large 27-1/2in (70cm) lady of the early 1860s with a simple hairdo. She has the rare feature of brown eyes, seldom found on china head dolls. She has beautiful sloping shoulders so that she can wear those fashionable dropped shoulder dresses of the 1860s. *H & J Foulke, Inc.*

WHERE WERE CHINA DOLLS MADE?

They were not made in an exotic place like China. They were made in the small villages of the German hills of Thüringia. The secrets of making porcelain were not discovered in the Western world until the early 1700s, when a German chemist discovered the formula for hard paste porcelain. In 1710, the Königliche Porzellan Manufaktur, best known by its famous initials K.P.M., of Meissen, Germany, was the first factory in the Western world to produce china. K.P.M. primarily produced expensive articles for royalty and the wealthy class. Other German scientists continued working until they too discovered the secret formula, which soon became widely known and so was no longer a secret. This allowed many small porcelain factories to open in the Thüringia area. It was a very good place for porcelain manufacturing because there were small towns where people needed to work, and the right natural resources were available: fine kaolin for making the porcelain and lots of wood from the forests to fuel the furnaces. Objects made of porcelain became very popular even with the middle class, who could afford to purchase the products of the smaller factories because they were less expensive than the products of the famous K.P.M. factory.

The Sonneberg area of Thüringia was already established in the toy and doll

17in (43cm) brown-haired man with pink-tinted complexion by the K.P.M. factory. The K.P.M. factory was founded in 1761 and was renowned for making very fine porcelain and very intricate figurines. Brown-haired china dolls are very seldom found. *Private Collection.*

A very nice boy of the 1880s from Alt, Beck & Gottschalck's mold 784, which is found in both blonde and black hair. His hair modeling is excellent with deep comb marks; his large blue eyes are distinctive of the ABG children. He has a beautiful lustrous complexion with a pink tint. *H & J Foulke, Inc.*

business at this time, having a rich tradition that by the early 1800s reached back hundreds of years. Whole villages based their economies on the toy trade. It seems inevitable that Thüringia's two prominent industries, porcelain and dolls, would mesh into an advantageous union. Other than its fragility, porcelain proved itself a wonderful medium for doll production and continued to be used for play dolls for more than 100 years. A few porcelain doll heads were produced in Copenhagen, and perhaps a few in France and England, but Germany was the main source of these interesting dolls.

Unfortunately, the majority of china doll heads are not marked as to maker. A few can be identified, and we have pointed these out in the descriptions accompanying the photographs. Although doll historians have identified names of porcelain factories that produced china heads, they have generally been unable to ascertain which unmarked heads were from a specific factory. According to listings in the Colemans' *The Collector's Encyclopedia of Dolls, Vol. II*, the following German porcelain factories made china dolls: Alt, Beck & Gottschalck (some incised with three or four digit mold number and size number); Bähr & Pröschild; Bohne Ernst; Conta & Boehme (shield mark inside shoulder plate); Dressel, Kister & Co.; William Goebel; Hertwig & Co. (pet names, probably others); Kestner & Co.; C.F. Kling & Co.; Kloster Veilsdorf (incised "Germany" and size number); K.P.M.; Orven, Knabe & Co. (used initials "O.K." on heads); F. Pfeffer; Theodor Pohl; Pollack & Hoffman; A.H. Pröschold; and Reideler & Wallendorf. Heads have been found with the "Pat. Dec 7/80" mark of the Bawo & Dotter doll factory.

What Are The Desirable Qualities Of China Head Dolls?

Hairdos.

The hairdos tell almost the whole story about china head dolls. The dolls with the early hairdos from the 1840s are the most desirable, the hardest to find and generally the most expensive. You will see numerous illustrations of these later in this book. Also desirable are the fancy hairdos from the late 1860s and 1870s. Fewer dolls were made with the very elaborate hairstyles, so they are harder to find, hence more expensive. You will also see many examples of these dolls later in this book.

Details in Hair.

Look for individual brush marks around the face, deep molding of curls, waves, braids, buns and so on. Also look for molded comb marks, which give the hair texture and a natural look. Any molded added details such as ribbons, flowers, snoods, combs, feathers or tassels add interest and are very desirable. Brown-haired dolls are seldom found, and blondes are rare during certain decades.

Decorating Details.

Look for an overall appealing face; a pink-tinted complexion is very desirable. Look for a red eyelid line over the eye, red dots at the eye corners and red nostril dots. A white space between the lips is unusual. A shading line between the lips of a darker color is attractive. There should be a black eyelash line over the eye. Look for an attractive eye color, perhaps even two-toned with

This 23in (58cm) lady of the 1860s has what I call a modified flat-top hairdo because it is gently rounded on the top instead of nearly flat across the top like some others. These types of chinas are plentiful enough that you should be able to find one with an exceptionally nice face like this doll's face. She has large blue eyes with red eyelid line and black eyelash line. Her very nice mouth has full upper and lower lips, even a shading line of a contrasting pink between them. *H & J Foulke, Inc.*

outlined iris, and a white dot highlight. Brown eyes are rarely found.

Modeling Details.

Look for molded eye sockets, sometimes even a molded eyelid, and good detail in the mouth. An open mouth would be rare. A molded necklace or a molded collar or blouse on the shoulder plate would be unusual. A molded necklace with a "gemstone" inset in the shoulder plate is also unusual. Pierced ears are a plus feature. The sharpest features will be seen on a doll made early in the life of the mold. As the mold gets older, the features are much softer. A mold can only be used for a certain number of pressings then it is replaced by another of the same design.

Quality.

Look for the best example that you can find of a style that you like. Without doubt you are going to find some imperfections in the making, some light peppering, a few pocks or pits. You will probably even find some wear on the hair. These things don't devalue the doll unless they are so prominent that they destroy your appreciation for the doll. You should, however, not settle for a doll with a mottled complexion.

Old Body.

Whenever possible an original or at least appropriate old body is most desirable. In most cases, a rule of thumb is that a new body devalues the doll by about 25-30%. A new body with old lower limbs is preferable to a totally new one. You want an old body which is appropriate for the head. For example, an 1840s head should not be on an 1890s printed cloth body with heeled boots.

Boots.

Black is usual for the molded boots and blue is usual for the painted garters, so look for boots that are different colors and for those that have good molding detail featuring gussets and buttons. Boots before 1870 should be flat-soled; boots after that time should be heeled.

Eyes.

In china head dolls blue eyes are usual. Brown eyes are rare, and so are glass eyes.

Swivel Neck.

A German china head doll with molded hair and swivel neck would be very rare.

Details on Cloth Bodies.

While many cloth bodies are plain, some have interesting construction details. Look for sewn-on corsets; striped, patterned or colored fabric on the lower leg to indicate stockings; applied garters; and sewn-on leather or oilcloth boots with tassels in front. Two companies that made bodies with these features are Bawo & Dotter in Germany and Philip Goldsmith in the United States.

THE 1840S – THE BEGINNING

It was during the 1840s that china head dolls began to be mass produced. Collectors refer to the china dolls of this decade as "early." They were made by various German porcelain factories, but only the K.P.M. factory in Germany and Royal Copenhagen in Denmark marked some of their dolls, so historians to date have not been able to identify the makers of most early china dolls. Dolls of this era are in great demand among collectors of china head dolls and, because of their rarity, prices are high. Most dolls shown in this section would be at least $3000 and many would be more.

Most of the 1840s china heads have black hair, but a few were made with brown hair, some of them coming from the K.P.M. factory. Some of these brown-haired dolls have their hair highlighted with darker brown strokes. Being both unusual and early, brown-haired dolls are very desirable to collectors. Dolls

of the 1840s were primarily ladies with contemporary hairstyles which featured molded buns, some quite intricately designed. Some of these dolls have exposed ears with the hair draping in

This 19in (48cm) brown-haired lady of the 1840s was produced by the Königliche Porzellan Manufaktur in Berlin, Germany. This company used the familiar blue or red stamped "K.P.M." initials on their dolls, but you have to look on the inside of the shoulder plate to find them. The quality of K.P.M. dolls is superb, with lustrous pink-tinted complexion and detailed molding in both the face and hair. *Private Collection.*

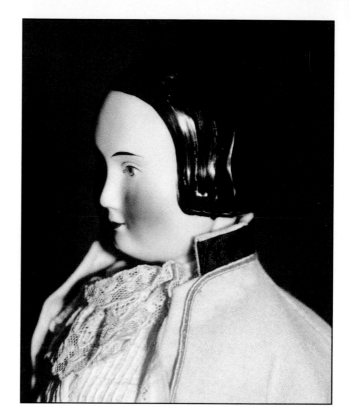

This 19in (48cm) man has side-parted black hair and a pink-tint complexion. Male china head dolls are considered rare. *Frances Walker Collection. Courtesy of Richard W. Withington, Inc.*

front of the ear and being combed to the back. The faces are very individual and look as though they might be portraits of real people. A few of them have pink-tinted complexions, which provide a more natural flesh color. A few have brown eyes. Both of these are desirable features.

The majority of 1840s dolls are on cloth bodies, some with china lower arms. Of course, it is always preferable to have an original or at least old body of the period. However, because fabric is a perishable material subject to deterioration from light, dirt and insects, it is becoming quite difficult to find early chinas on original bodies. Some trade-offs have to be made in collecting old dolls, and perhaps this is one.

A few of the early china heads are found on jointed pegwood bodies with china lower limbs. A wood body adds value to this type of doll. If you are considering one, be sure that it has its correct china lower limbs. It is better to have the originals, even if they are repaired, than wood-carved replacements.

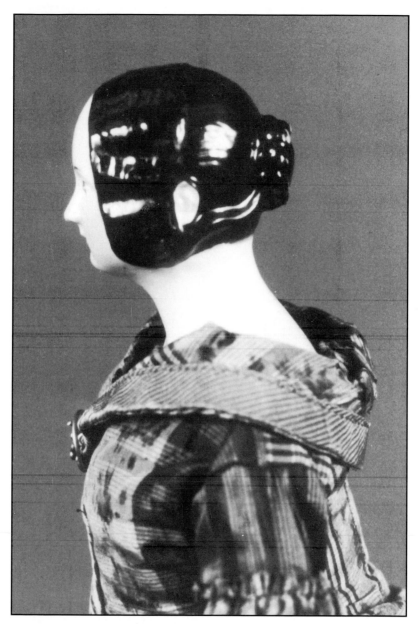

OPPOSITE PAGE AND ABOVE: Pink-tinted complexion and very strong facial modeling are two desirable features on this 19in (48cm) lady. The profile view shows her exposed ears. This hairdo, of which many variations are known, is referred to by collectors as "Queen Victoria," but it is unlikely that it is actually a portrait doll. Victoria came to the English throne in 1837, and, as shown in the many paintings of her, she did wear this hairstyle. *Private Collection.*

This dark-haired doll has the unidentified mark "T.P.M." She is another variation of the "Queen Victoria" hairstyle but with less molding in the hair and more exposure to the ear. She is wearing a very nice period dress. *Private Collection.*

In lovely all original condition, this 21in (53cm) lady has a braided bun hairdo and pink-tinted complexion. *H & J Foulke, Inc.*

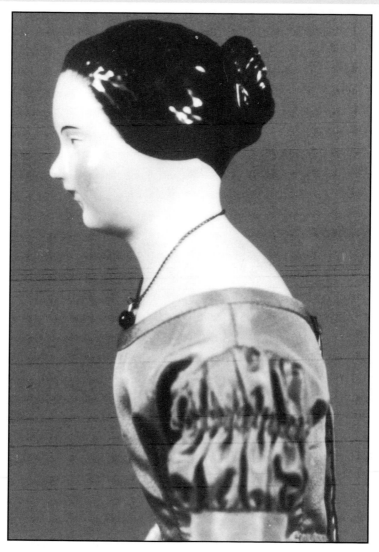

OPPOSITE PAGE AND ABOVE: This lady has a very Germanic look, softened by the pink-tint complexion and the tiny brush strokes around her face to indicate individual hairs. The side view shows her very interesting profile. *Private Collection.*

A very delicate face and molded bun in an unusually high position make this 14in (36cm) lady very desirable. Faces are so distinctive on many of these early chinas that they appear to have been sculpted from real people. *Richard Wright Antiques.*

This stunning aristocratic lady has her hair waved back over her ears into braids wrapped around her head and held in place by a large molded tortoise shell comb. This 6-1/2in (17cm) head alone (no body) brought over $10,000 at auction in June 1993. *Frances Walker Collection. Courtesy of Richard W. Withington, Inc.*

Dolls had always been primarily ladies, with a few males, but some child or *Kinderkopf* were produced in the 1840s and 1850s. They are characterized by short necks, round faces and short wind-blown hairstyles with brush marks – or, as in the doll shown here, strands of hair painted around the faces. The *Kinderkopf* heads could be either girls or boys, although this one definitely looks like a boy. This doll has a particularly strong face with molded eyelid, a prominent philtrum and lips going almost into a smile, as well as rarely found brown eyes. It is a choice example. *Frances Walker Collection. Courtesy of Richard W. Withington, Inc.*

OPPOSITE PAGE AND ABOVE: This 13in (33cm) china doll has a molded white bonnet with ruffles around her face and fuchsia ribbon and bow. Early bonnet dolls are desirable and rare. For an early doll with a totally different white bonnet, see my ***Doll Classics,*** page 133. *Candace Doelman Collection. Courtesy of Richard W. Withington, Inc.*

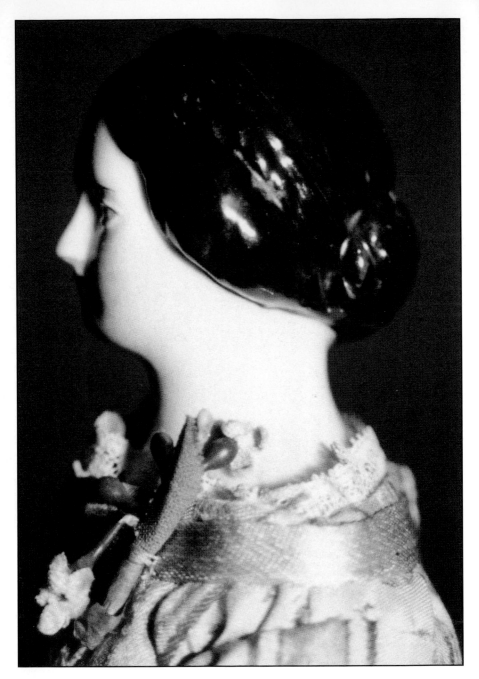

An unusual 15in (38cm) lady with brown hair waved into braids circling her head and forming a low double-braided bun. *Frances Walker Collection. Courtesy of Richard W. Withington, Inc.*

This 13in (33cm) lady is a lovely example of the work of the Royal Copenhagen Manufactory in Denmark. She has brown hair waved over her ears into a high soft bun with a curl on her neck behind each ear. According to the Colemans' *The Collector's Encyclopedia of Dolls*, Royal Copenhagen produced china doll heads from the 1840s to the 1880s, but their output was only about 23,000 heads, nearly all being made before 1860. Royal Copenhagen china heads were marked inside the shoulder plate with the traditional R.C. mark of three lines. Within the past 20 years, three heads have been reissued; these have modern R.C. markings. It is prudent to be cautious and to make sure an R.C. doll is an antique before purchasing it. *Candace Doelman Collection. Courtesy of Richard W. Withington, Inc.*

THE 1850S — THE DECADE OF INNOVATIONS

Production of china head dolls really picked up in the 1850s, but it still wasn't booming. Several important innovations were introduced during this decade. China head dolls were outfitted with real hair wigs; they were given glass eyes; babies were made; and the extremely popular *badekinder*, or bathing dolls, were introduced.

As contemporary hairstyles changed, so did those of the china head dolls. Some designs continued to be made for years, but generally when new designs were created, they were given hairstyles that real ladies were wearing at that time.

This 19in (48cm) pink-tint china head has the desirable "covered-wagon" hairstyle with center part, smooth crown and all round finger curls. She is an outstanding example of her type with lovely molded eye sockets, rare brown eyes and wonderfully appealing face. She is totally original. *Yvonne Baird Collection.*

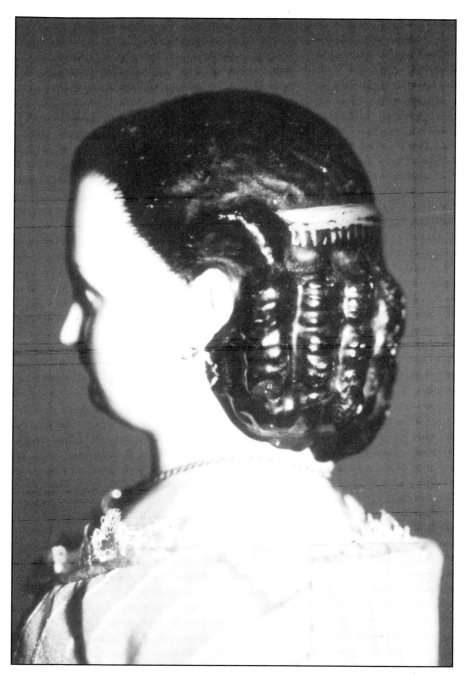

This doll has a variation of the covered-wagon hairdo with the interesting feature of a gold lustre band just above her back curls. Brush marks frame her face and pierced-in ears hold earrings. She is 14in (36cm). *Frances Walker Collection. Courtesy of Richard W. Withington, Inc.*

PREVIOUS PAGE AND ABOVE: This is a great doll, but very difficult to place in time; however, I think she fits this period because of her strong face. We have to keep in mind that some of these molds were used for 20 or 30 years, so dating is sometimes guess work. Her hair is brushed back from her face as indicated by the tiny brush marks showing exquisite detail. This special decoration took much more time than simply painting a wave. Her profile view shows her prominent nose and emphasizes her long neck. Her hair is pulled into a low loose bun on her neck. *Private Collection.*

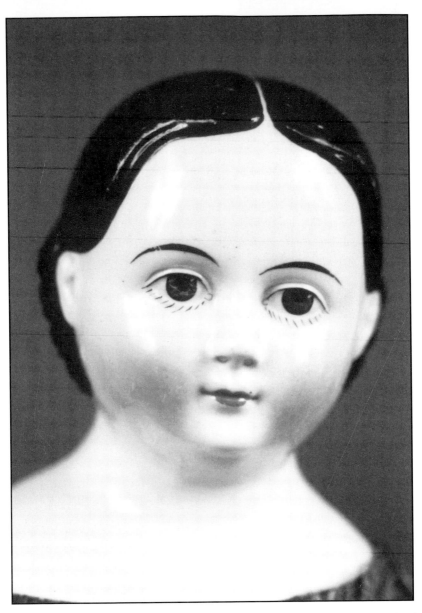

A 20in (51cm) doll with pink-tinted complexion and large brown eyes; note the tiny painted lower eyelashes typical with this very appealing face. From her white center part her hair is combed down and back into short sausage curls. This is called a "Greiner-style" hairdo because it is found on the 1858 papier-mâché dolls from the Greiner firm in Philadelphia. She is excellent quality and very desirable. This face can also be found with different hairstyles: waves down each side of the face or hair straight across the forehead pulled back into a hairband. *H & J Foulke, Inc.*

This 15in (38cm) doll is an example of a very desirable model with Greiner-style hairdo and glass eyes. Notice her painted upper and lower eyelashes. Glass-eyed chinas are rare. *Candace Doelman Collection. Courtesy of Richard W. Withington, Inc.*

This 14in (36cm) china has an unusual hairdo for a glass-eyed china. She is dressed in old print cotton fabric, which seems especially appropriate for her plain hairdo. Wearing her requisite apron, she is a member of her owner's "kitchen brigade," which occupies a nook in a special corner of the kitchen. *Private Collection.*

A 9in (23cm) täu-fling-type china doll, having brown molded hair in the so-called "Alice" style pulled back from her face with a molded hair band. She has the same type of body as the doll on page 43. *H & J Foulke, Inc.*

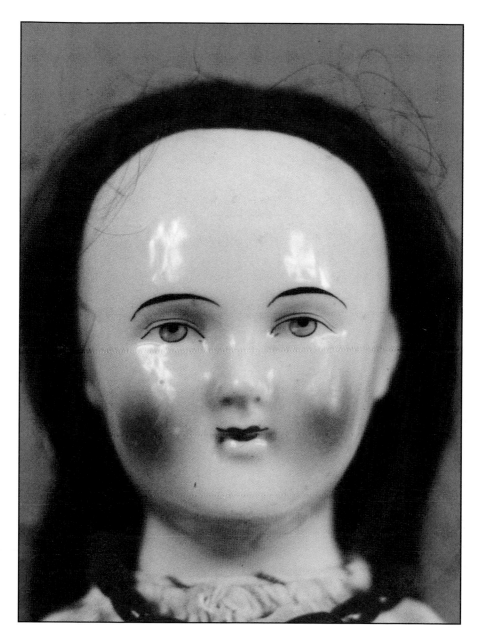

This type of china head is called a bald head, a Biedermeier, or a "black spot" china. She has a bald head with a black painted spot on top, and was meant to have a real hair wig. The original wigs still in the original set are very desirable on these types of dolls, but most of them by now have lost their original curls. No one is sure just what the purpose of the black spot was. This lady is 17in (43cm) tall with a slightly pink complexion. *H & J Foulke, Inc.*

A 13in (33cm) very unusual and innovative bald head china with glass sleeping eyes. Some dolls of this type have painted eyelashes. Her wig and hat are inappropriate and should be replaced, but we were happy to have her photograph anyway because she is rare. Actually, with the sleeping eyes, she probably is a later date than the 1850s, but no one is really sure. *Candace Doelman Collection. Courtesy of Richard W. Withington, Inc.*

OPPOSITE PAGE: Left: The 9in (23cm) china baby doll was an invention of the 1850s. The doll was also produced in papier-mâché and became quite popular, but the china version is rarely found. The head swivels on a china shoulder plate; the lower arms, hips and lower legs all are china. The midsection and upper limbs are twill cloth with a voice box in the torso. This type of body was supposedly copied from a Japanese doll that one of the German dollmakers saw at an exhibition in London. On some of these china täuflings the shoulder plate and hips are papier-mâché instead of china. Some babies are found with short molded hair like this one; some have bald heads with painted wisps of hair. *H & J Foulke, Inc.*

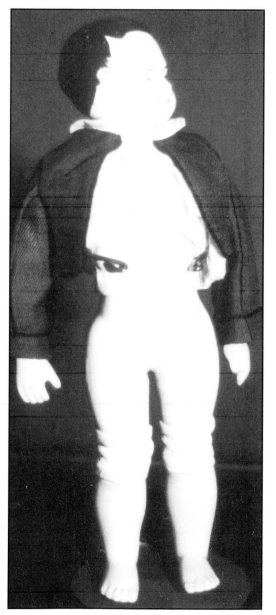

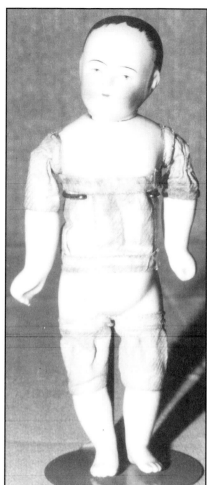

ABOVE: Another 9in (23cm) täu-fling-type china doll but with very unusual hip section with long upper legs, leather midsection and knees. This is the only one of this type that I have ever seen. *Frances Walker Collection. Courtesy of Richard W. Withington, Inc.*

THE 1860S — PLAIN AND PLENTIFUL

Dividing the study of china head dolls into periods of ten years is an arbitrary way of examining a production that covered 80 or 90 years. There is no exact cut-off date known for any specific hairdo, and, the German dollmakers being well known for cost cutting, each hairdo was probably used until it was hopelessly out of fashion and customers demanded a more up-to-date style. So, we have grouped the china head dolls according to

This 19in (48cm) lady has wavy hair around her face and three rows of soft, short curls in the back. Her mouth is very well modeled with individual lips, even a white space between them, which is unusual for a china. This face is sometimes found with brown eyes. *H & J Foulke, Inc.*

This 14-1/2in (37cm) lady is a lovely example of an 1860s doll with several desirable qualities. Her complexion has a faint pink tint, and her painting is very well done. Moreover, she has her original cloth body with its china lower limbs and painted black flat-soled boots, which are correct for dolls of this period. She is completely original in her white dress with pink ribbon insertion and cream cotton panties, shirt and petticoat. Since her dress hem falls just below her knee, I think she represents a child. During this period, few actual child dolls were made. *H & J Foulke, Inc.*

This 19in (48cm) doll has especially large eyes, nicely painted with a red eyelid line. She has a "younger" look to her face, which is particularly appealing. *Dolly Valk Collection.*

what appear to be the prevalent hairstyles of the decades, also taking into consideration what we feel are probably characteristics of production during that decade. Some of the grouping, of course, is guess work, supposition and deductive reasoning.

Apparently the German china doll came into her own during the 1860s, and production reached its peak. Very few of these dolls are found today in Germany, as they were made primarily for export, mostly to the United States. These simple hairdos seem to be particularly fitting for the United States, which was involved in its terrible Civil War from 1861-1865. There was little cause for frivolity on either side. The chinas of the 1860s had pure white complexions with rosy apple cheeks, vivid blue painted eyes and shiny black hair with a center part. On first fleeting look, it seems as though all of these ladies are the same, but closer examination and comparison reveals that there are over 30 different models of these ladies.

The availability of these 1860s chinas makes them a good place for interested collectors to enter the china market because the prices are in the $200-400 range, except for those in the largest sizes. Many collectors, appreciating the charm inherent in some of these wonderful old ladies, also realize the good value they are getting for their collecting dollar. The dolls are antiques in the true sense of the word, being well over 100 years old. Ever since I have been into dolls, the chinas have been on a slowly upward swing. There has been no great boom, just a gentle rise – and never a decline. Collectors who love chinas are glad to be in a field that is not so popular that the prices skyrocket. In fact, it is often possible to buy chinas for below so-called "book price" because they are not in as great demand as the bisque dolls.

Another black-haired doll with a slightly "younger" look. In dressing dolls, the scale of design in lace and fabrics should be considered. I think the design in this lace is much too large for this doll. *H & J Foulke, Inc.*

Seldom is a blonde-haired doll found in this period, so this doll is fairly unusual. She has a very broad forehead with simple soft curls. This hairstyle also comes in black, but it is not found as often as the flat-top style. *H & J Foulke, Inc.*

This attractive 21-1/2in (55cm) lady has a simple hairdo with 13 sausage curls all the way around. The molding of her hair shows deep comb marks, which is a desirable detail. *H & J Foulke, Inc.*

A 20in (51cm) lady with flat-top hairdo and very nice facial expression. Her large blue eyes have molded eyelids and a red upper eyelid line. It is her mouth that is interesting, with deeply molded, yet thinly painted, upper lip with upturned corners and an oval lower lip, which does not even fill out the molded area. *H & J Foulke, Inc.*

Here is a doll with a name, "Adelina Patti." Her hairstyle is characterized by brush stroked sides representing individual hairs brushed back into soft curls. Her small lips are painted individually with a small white space between them. *H & J Foulke, Inc.*

A 23in (58cm) blonde-haired lady with a flat-top hairdo and sausage curls. It is unusual to find this hairstyle in blonde. Notice the brown eyebrows used with the light hair. *H & J Foulke, Inc.*

This 24in (61cm) lady has the same hairdo as the doll pictured on page 51, but it is interesting to note the different faces. Much variation occurs because the faces are hand-painted, and changes in a small detail can change the face.

Eyes could be made larger or smaller; cheeks could be lighter or darker. The mouth has a lot to do with expression. Sometimes the upper lip is turned up or down, and the lower lip can be larger or smaller. *H & J Foulke, Inc.*

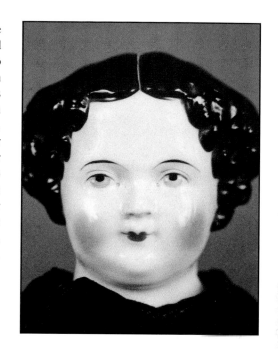

Of course, many cloth bodies simply disintegrated over the past 130 years, so many china heads are found as heads only. Some people like to make them new bodies and dress them; some collectors like to find them old bodies; some just leave them as heads! This boy or child doll has short hair with nice brush-mark detailing around the face, giving him a wind-blown look. His complexion is light pink; eyes are deep blue with white highlight, even shading around the iris. His slightly parted lips are the same color as his nostril dots and eyelid line. As to his date, we really are not sure; he could just as easily have been put in the section with the 1850 dolls, but it is nice to have a boy in this section also. *Frances Walker Collection. Courtesy of Richard W. Withington, Inc.*

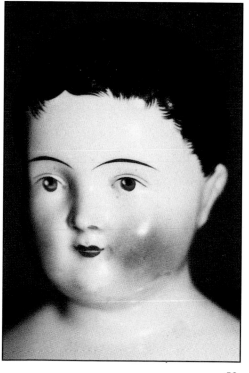

These dolls are 7-1/2in (19cm) and 9-1/2in (24cm) tall. They have what collectors refer to as the "flat-top" hairdo. As happens with many of the small dolls, the painting detail is not so fine as on the larger dolls. However, their redeeming quality is that they are totally original in their store clothes. It is helpful to see how many of these dolls were originally dressed so that those without clothes can be attired in the correct style and fabric. Both dolls have their original china limbs and feet with painted black flat-soled boots. *H & J Foulke, Inc.*

THE 1860s AND 1870s — FANCY AND EMBELLISHED

Not all of the ladies wore plain hair throughout the 1860s. There were many fancy hairstyles. Some of these ladies must have had enormously long hair to have achieved such styles. Of course, they also used rats and buns for padding, as well as supplementing their own hair with additional hair pieces. Snoods became popular. I think this would be a very convenient way to cope with a lot of hair when there was no time to get it into one of those fancy "dos." I would suspect that snoods were often worn around the house. Some of the snoods had ruffles, feathers, bows and flowers across the crowns. China head dolls with molded and painted or lustre snoods are very desirable. Some dolls have molded snoods that were not painted. These are nice, but the painted ones are better. This is also the period when hairdos were embellished with flowers, beads, ribbons and frills. Some dolls were given pierced ears, molded necklaces or molded shoulder plates. All of these unusual features are very desirable.

This doll is by far one of the most beautiful and desirable of china heads. She is called "Morning Glory" because of the flowers that she has molded and painted behind her ears. The hair is pulled back from the face showing many individual brush strokes into a braided bun with some loose hair falling down the back of the neck. "Morning Glory" comes with either black or brown hair and complexion tinting ranging from light to heavy. She is 21in (53cm) tall. *Richard Wright Antiques.*

A 14in (36cm) lady with very nice hairstyle but with the very unusual features for a china head doll of a molded bodice with collar and glass eyes. She is extremely rare. *Private Collection.*

A lovely 21in (53cm) lady with a molded gold lustre snood and beautiful detail in hair painting, with brush strokes at the temples. She has a long curl hanging down each side of her neck. *Private Collection.*

A front view of another doll with the same hairdo. *Richard Wright Antiques.*

ABOVE AND OPPOSITE PAGE: This lovely lady is another rare one. Her blonde hair is puffed out on the sides then pulled to the back in long curls held by a band of beads. Also notice her molded necklace and the incredible detail in the modeling of the hair, including curls and comb marks.

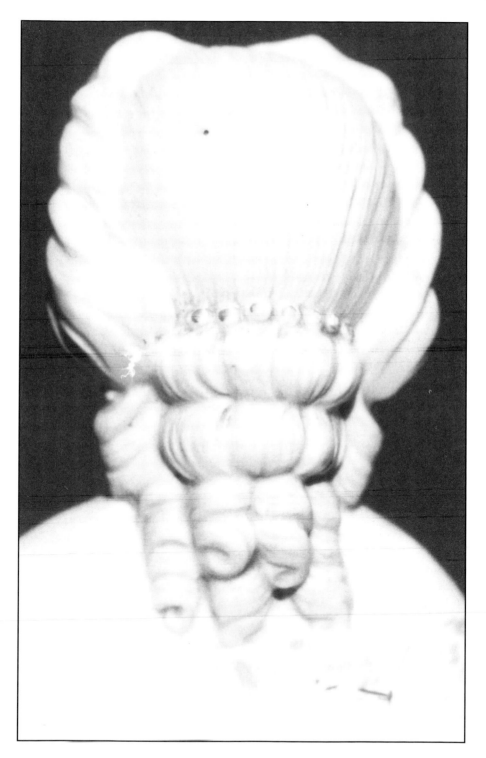

Another doll of the same mold, showing the side and back of her hair. It's almost impossible to think that this elaborate doll was made as a child's plaything. She brought $3900 at auction in June 1993. *Frances Walker Collecton. Courtesy of Richard W. Withington, Inc.*

PREVIOUS PAGE: A stunning 17in (43cm) blonde-haired lady of incredible detail with hair pulled away from her face and held by a blue ribbon. Notice the pierced ears, unusual on a china doll. *Private Collection.*

Brown-haired dolls from this period are very rare. This lady has the same hairdo as the two dolls shown on page 57 with the nice details of brush marks at her temples and a gold lustre bow and snood. *Richard Wright Antiques.*

This 11-1/2in (29cm) tall lady with blonde hair has a black molded and painted snood held in place by a blue fluted ribbon which gives the appearance of a crown. *Private Collection.*

ABOVE AND OPPOSITE PAGE: Two views of a very popular doll named "Mary Todd." Certainly it is doubtful that this is a portrait of President Lincoln's wife, but at least it is in the right period. This is an especially pretty example with gold lustre ribbons and snood. *Sheila Needle.*

This 23-1/2in (60cm) tall doll is referred to as "Young Victoria." This is complete-ly a misnomer because Victoria was born in 1819, so by the mid 1860s she could hardly be described as young! Whatever the name, this is a lovely doll with braids encircling her head. *Jackson/Pearson Collection.*

A lovely 21in (53cm) lady with pierced ears, brush marks framing her face and hair pulled back into a cascade of high curls. *Jackson/Pearson Collection.*

19in (48cm) lady with fancy hairdo containing molded beads which are not decorated; brush marks frame her face and exposed ears. *Frances Walker Collection. Courtesy of Richard W. Withington, Inc.*

A 21in (53cm) lady marked "B 22" with very high hairdo and two curls falling down the nape of the neck as well as pierced ears. Sometimes it pays to take a look at the back and sides of a china head for details that can't be seen from the front. *Frances Walker Collection. Courtesy of Richard W. Withington, Inc.*

This 17in (43cm) lady has a hairstyle very similar to the 1840s dolls except the bun with coiled braids is much looser, and there is an additional braid across the top of her head. She is wearing her original green taffeta dress. *H & J Foulke, Inc.*

A 21in (53cm) lady with a lovely complexion. Her blonde hair is loosely braided on the sides and trimmed with two rows of molded beads. *Private Collection.*

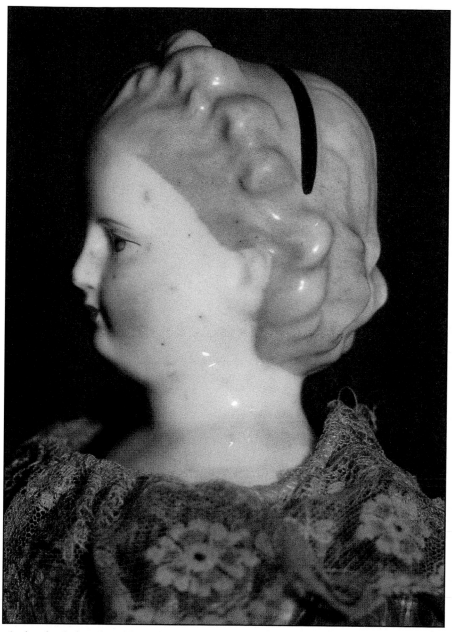

A simpler hairstyle with molded curls framing her face and a painted and molded black hairband. She is 16in (41cm) tall. *Frances Walker Collection. Courtesy of Richard W. Withington, Inc.*

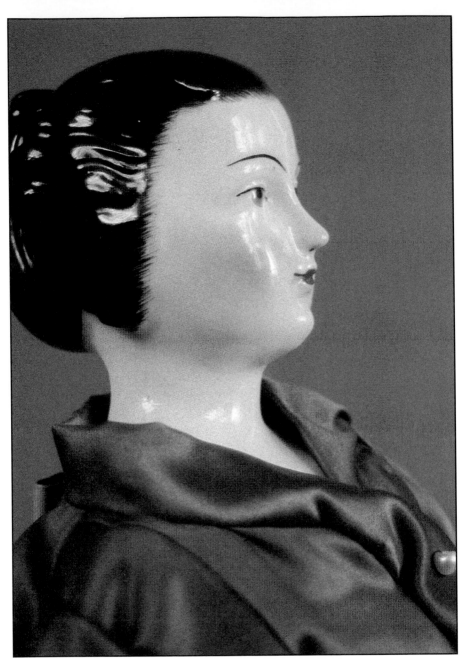

This beautiful lady with pink-tint complexion is 24in (61cm) tall. She has brush marks all around her face with hair combed flat on top, puffed out on the sides and brought back into a twisted bun with a smooth portion of back hair tucked up into it. *H & J Foulke, Inc.*

A 22-1/2in (57cm) lady with excellent modeling including pierced ears, this doll has a very attractive face. Her hair has lots of molding detail including comb marks, brush strokes at temples and a heavy braid encircling her head. An identical doll is known to have inside her shoulders the mark of Conta & Boehme, Possneck, Thüringia, Germany, who also are known to have made Frozen Charlottes. She also is documented with blonde hair. *Frances Walker Collection. Courtesy of Richard W. Withington, Inc.*

This small 14in (37cm) very unusual china head has the look of a younger lady. Her hair, with brush strokes at the temples, is pulled to the top of her head in a roll, then curled to the back in short waves. *H & J Foulke, Inc.*

This pretty 16in (42cm) lady has light brown hair, called *café-au-lait* by collectors, in the style known as "curly top." This head is also found with black hair. *H & J Foulke, Inc.*

THE 1880s — CHILDREN

A new type of china head doll entered the scene in the 1880s — the child. While, as we have seen, there had been a few *Kinderkopf*, china-hipped children, Frozen Charlies and dolls with youthful faces, the 1880s saw the first widespread manufacturing of child dolls. Perhaps part of the interest in child china dolls was due to the development in the doll world of the bisque child doll, which came on the scene in France in 1878 and quickly travelled to Germany. Whatever the impetus, after 40 years of primarily lady dolls, the scene was changing.

The new child china heads were modeled with round, chubby faces and short necks. The hairstyles were short – sometimes with bangs and often with curls. The eyes are larger and painted more dramatically as befits the wonder of childhood. Many dolls of this period have been incorrectly dressed as ladies and men because their collectors were not aware that these dolls were meant to be children.

Best of all for curious collectors, we have the emergence of

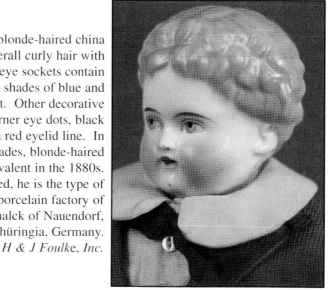

A 20-1/2in (52cm) blonde-haired china head boy with overall curly hair with bangs. His molded eye sockets contain large irises with two shades of blue and white dot highlight. Other decorative features are red corner eye dots, black eyelash line and a red eyelid line. In contrast to earlier decades, blonde-haired chinas were quite prevalent in the 1880s.

Although unmarked, he is the type of doll produced by the porcelain factory of Alt, Beck & Gottschalck of Nauendorf, near Ohrdruf, Thüringia, Germany.
H & J Foulke, Inc.

marks on the back of the shoulder plates on some of these dolls, which helps us identify specific models and a few makers. However, many china heads still remained unmarked.

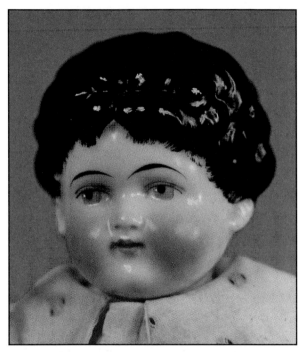

This black-haired boy is from the same mold as the preceding doll, also unmarked. Notice the individual brush strokes on his forehead. He is 20in (51 cm) tall. Sometimes ABG dolls can be found with their original factory china lower limbs. The lower arms have cupped hands with a separately molded thumb. The legs have black-heeled boots which come to a "V" in front. Having original factory limbs would be a plus factor for an ABG doll. *H & J Foulke, Inc.*

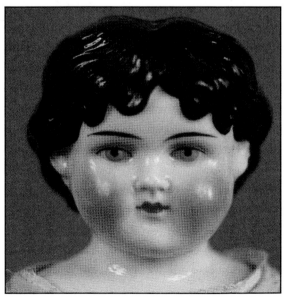

This 17in (43cm) girl is by Alt, Beck & Gottschalck from their mold 1046. Most of these children can be either boys or girls. Her hair is molded with nice comb marks and curls falling onto her forehead. This mold also comes with blonde hair. ABG dolls from this period are marked across the back shoulder plate in a distinctive way. *H & J Foulke, Inc.*

Another head by ABG with overall black curly hair and exposed ears. This one is a large 28in (71cm) size. *H & J Foulke, Inc.*

This pretty blonde-haired child is from mold 189 by Kling & Co. and has their trademark "K" in a bell on the bottom back shoulder plate. This head often comes with a pink-tinted complexion. The hairstyle is simple, with center part and short curls; it also comes with black hair. The brown eyebrows are quite thick for a china doll; she has no red eyelid line, inner eye dots or nostril dots. *H & J Foulke, Inc.*

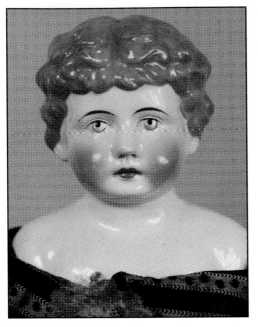

Although she is dressed as a lady, I think she looks more like a child. She is unmarked, but her eyes are in the ABG style. The face is quite different from her brothers and sisters in that she has very long cheeks and her mouth has a downturned upper lip. When collecting china heads, always be on the lookout for a different and unusual face. *H & J Foulke, Inc.*

A very nice boy of the 1880s from Alt, Beck & Gottschalck's mold 784, which is found in both blonde and black hair. Hair modeling is excellent with deep comb marks; his large blue eyes are distinctive of ABG; beautiful complexion. *H & J Foulke, Inc.*

A nice china head with wide forehead and overall curls with good depth to the molding. Sometimes when a mold is overused, little detail is left in the hair modeling, but this one is very good. Her lips are nicely done; the upper one is painted with upturned corners. She has an old homemade body entirely of cloth, which is what I refer to as a "clunker." Probably done without a pattern, it has impossibly out of proportion arms and legs. I love these types of bodies because they are so folksy! She is 24in (61cm) tall. *H & J Foulke, Inc.*

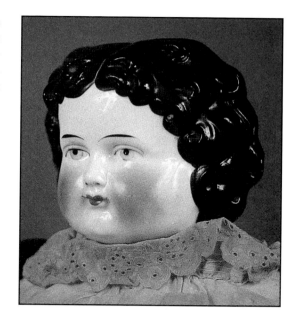

Here is the same mold with unusual blonde hair, in an 18in (46cm) size. Some heads of this type are marked with the Bawo & Dotter mark "Pat. Dec. 7/80" on the back shoulder plate. These marked heads would originally have been on the Dotter patented bodies with printed corsets. *H & J Foulke, Inc.*

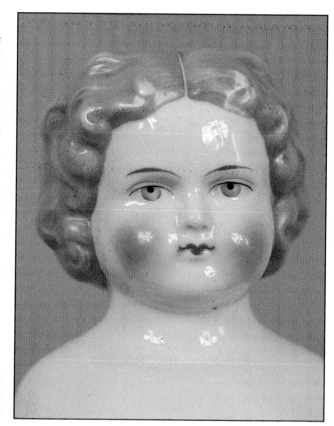

THE 1890S TO 1930S — WAVY HAIR AND PET NAMES

The last group of china head dolls was developed in the 1890s. Their hair was simple, just waves with or without a center part. The quality was not as good as previous dolls. People with money to spend on dolls were buying French and German bisque dolls. The china head dolls had lost favor, but they still filled a niche in the market for cheap dolls. This style of doll was sold until the 1930s. Most heads of the 1890s are of unknown manufacture, but some are marked simply "Germany" in accordance with the 1891 import law.

A 20in (51cm) lady with hairstyle typical of the 1890s. Actually, for this late date she is of very nice quality with a smooth white complexion, white center part to her hair, deeply molded waves, red eyelid line, black eyelash line and nicely painted mouth. *H & J Foulke, Inc.*

 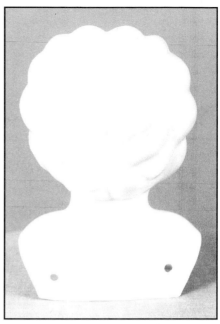

Blonde-haired shoulder head of the 1890s with pale blue eyes, red eyelid line and black eyelash line. The holes in the shoulder plate are for sewing the head to the cloth body. Collectors consider the blondes of the 1890s to be more desirable than the black-haired dolls. While there may be fewer blondes during this period, they are not rare. *H & J Foulke, Inc.*

The china heads with names are very popular with collectors. These dolls were sold by Butler Brothers but were made in Germany for them by Hertwig & Co. They were issued about 1899 and continued in production for 30 years. The dolls came with either blonde or black hair, with one third being blonde. They had a molded blouse with collar and name with applied gold trim. Sizes varied from 7-1/2in (19cm) up. Some of the dolls had printed cloth bodies with ABCs, flags, numbers, and so on. These make an interesting collection in themselves. The Pet Name dolls have factory cloth bodies with china lower limbs, the foot having a black-heeled boot and the calf having a blue painted garter. The smaller dolls often had bisque limbs with no garter and brown boots. *Agnes* is 8in (20cm) tall. *H & J Foulke, Inc.*

Names used on the Pet Name dolls were *Agnes, Bertha, Daisy, Dorothy, Edith, Esther, Ethel, Florence, Helen, Mabel, Marion, Pauline* and *Ruth.* This 6in (15cm) head will make into about a 24in (61cm) doll. Her name is *Ruth. H & J Foulke, Inc.*

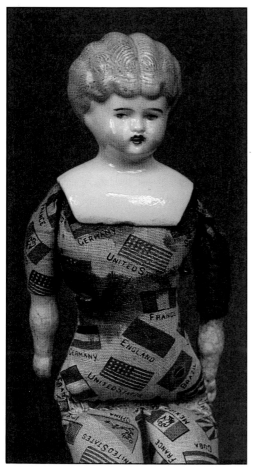

Although this is a late doll, it is very rare to find a china with open mouth and molded teeth. According to Angione & Wharton in their book *All Dolls Are Collectible*, Butler Brothers advertised this doll in 1908 with the body design called "Flags of All Nations." She is 10-1/2in (27cm) tall. *Private Collection.*

This delicate china head is from the German firm of Dressel & Kister, better known for their pincushion or half dolls. She is one from a series of shoulder head chinas with fancy hairdos and brush strokes over painted hair. These dolls have beautifully modeled arms and hands. They were likely created as ornamental dolls, not really playthings, and are often found in half form as for a boudoir lamp or candy box. This lovely lady is 13in (33cm) tall. *Candace Doelman Collection. Courtesy of Richard W. Withington, Inc.*

BATHING DOLLS OR FROZEN CHARLOTTES

An important type of all-china doll new to the 1850s was the bathing doll or *badekinder*, literally "bathing child." Collectors today call these dolls Frozen Charlottes or Frozen Charlies because their limbs do not move but are frozen in place. In spite of the fact that these dolls were unlikely playthings because of their fragility, they became extremely popular as attested to by the quantities of them still available today and by the fact that they were on the market for about 65 years. Over the years they were made in a large number of factories in sizes from one inch

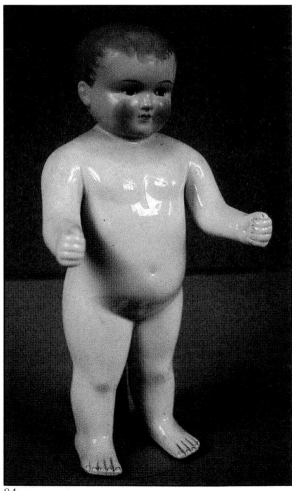

A 13-1/2in (34cm) Frozen Charlie of the type manufactured by Conta & Boehme, Possneck, Thüringia, Germany. Their shield mark is often found on the foot of these dolls. This desirable example has a pink-tinted head with blonde molded and painted hair showing individual brush strokes around the face. The painting of the eyes is beautifully detailed. His fingers and toes are individually molded with incised fingernails. *H & J Foulke, Inc.*

(3 centimeter) to 16 inches (41 centimeter). Hairstyles varied with the decades of production. Some of these dolls had molded bonnets, clothes or shoes. Good quality Frozen Charlottes are as popular with collectors today as they were with consumers years ago.

Once in a great while, an all-china doll is found with

A lovely 5in (13cm) Charlotte with complete pink-tint body complexion. Most Charlottes of this type have black hair in a covered-wagon hairdo, but this one is quite rare as she has a molded white bonnet with ruffled brim; it is trimmed with a painted rose ribbon and has rose ribbon ties under her chin. Some Charlottes have molded clothes instead of bonnets. These are also very collectible. *H & J Foulke, Inc.*

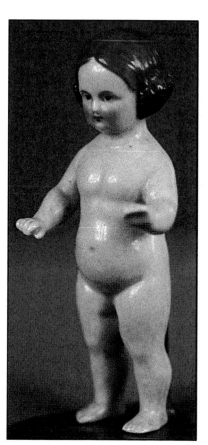

Very nice pink-tinted girl from the 1850s with cafe-au-lait hair in a covered-wagon hairdo. This color is rarely found in this style. She has very nice chubby modeling on her body. *H & J Foulke, Inc.*

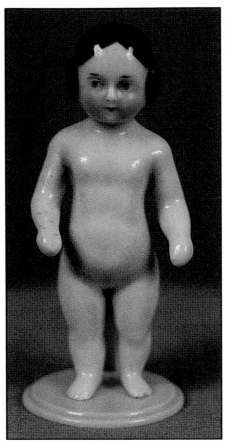

4-3/4in (12cm) Frozen Charlotte with covered-wagon hairdo and white complexion. These Charlottes of the 1850s represent toddlers and have very chubby bodies. *H & J Foulke, Inc.*

5-1/2in (14cm) all-china doll with short black hair could be used as either a girl or boy. It has a very nicely painted face with good detail and the chubby body modeling of an 1860s doll. *H & J Foulke, Inc.*

jointed shoulders and hips. These are usually from the 1860s period and are very desirable because of their rarity. An example is shown in Merrill's *The Art of Dolls*, page 133.

5-1/2in (14cm) Frozen Charlotte with blonde molded hair of the 1870s. She has a molded ribbon on her crown, which is hard to see because it is painted the same color as her hair. This frequently happens with decorations in the hair of china head dolls. Sometimes no time was taken to paint the decorations another color. Of course, this would have necessitated another firing, hence increasing the cost of production. She seems to be an older child because her limbs are not as chubby. *H & J Foulke, Inc.*

FOR FURTHER READING

Books

Borger, Mona. *China Dolls for Study and Admiration.* San Francisco: Borger Publications, 1983.

Merrill, Madeline. *The Art of Dolls.* Cumberland, MD: Hobby House Press, Inc., 1985.

Richter, Lydia. *China, Parian & Bisque German Dolls.* Cumberland, MD: Hobby House Press, Inc., 1993.

Magazine Articles

Foulke, Jan. "German China Dolls," *Doll Reader®*, May 1993.

Johnston, Estelle. "Cherishable China Dolls, Parts I & II." *Doll Reader®*, February/March 1985 and April 1985.

Langlois, Virginia. "Whence Came the Name?" *Doll News*, Spring 1990.

Nobel, John Darcy. "Plain & Fancy: A Historical Celebration of China Dolls." *Dolls*, May/June 1985.

Walker, Frances. "When China was Queen," *Doll News*, Fall 1989.

French China *Poupées*

Even a small book on china dolls would not be complete without mention of the lovely china *poupées* or lady dolls of the 1850s and 1860s which were made in France. Mlles Huret and Rohmer are the two famous names which come to mind when thinking of French china *poupées*. Dolls from both of these houses are well respected by collectors of dolls of this type. Since the china *poupées* are fairly difficult to find, I assume their production period was probably very short. A more plentiful supply of identical dolls can be found in bisque, leading to the conclusion that the matte complexion of the bisque proved more satisfactory at providing a life-like appearance than china with its shiny glaze. Although the china *poupées* were French dolls, the exact origin of their heads is still questionable. Many doll historians feel that some, if not all, of them are German products made to exact specifications for the French shops. There is no doubt that the bodies were made in France, most of leather or

A 14in (36cm) china *poupée* with beautiful pink-tinted complexion and dark glass eyes. *Jackie Kaner.*

leather and wood. The dolls usually have stout, curved one-piece china arms from mid upperarm to fingers, which are either separated or cupped; a few have china lower legs with bare feet. Many are stamped with the maker's name on the body. Although most of these dolls were dressed as ladies, a few were dressed as children or young ladies.

The heads themselves are very different from the usual German heads, which had solid domes even if they were outfitted with wigs. These French chinas had pates cut off diagonally, leaving a cavity to be covered by a cork pate. This allowed easy access for setting in glass eyes and, when outfitted with a cork pate, provided a place to nail on a wig, many of which were made from goat skin or mohair. The eyes were either glass

This 15in (38cm) French china *poupée* is a choice example with her original skin wig and clothing. She is on a pink kid body. *Candace Doelman Collection. Courtesy of Richard W. Withington, Inc.*

or beautifully painted with shaded irises, a black eyelash line and painted upper and lower eyelashes. Some dolls have swivel necks, an innovation which was patented by Mlle Huret in 1861. As for pricing, you can expect to pay $3000 and upward for a French china with perfect head, good body and appropriate clothing.

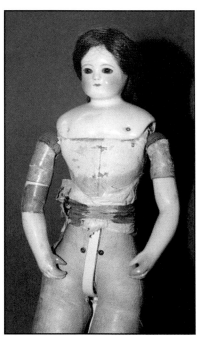

16in (41cm) china *poupée* appears to be on a Rohmer body which has typical wood upper arms with special joints at shoulders that allow the arms to maintain position rather than just flopping down at her sides; note her lovely 3/4 china arms. The two holes in her lower torso held tapes which either held up her stockings or helped position her legs for sitting. *Private Collection.*

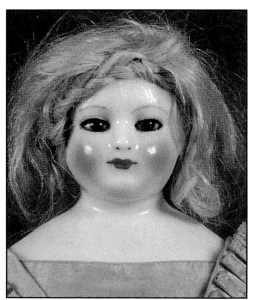

17in (43cm) china *poupée* shoulder head with characteristic almond-shaped glass eyes outlined with black eyeliner and accented with tiny painted eyelashes. Her face is nearly round with particularly rosy cheeks. She has a kid over wood body with curved 3/4 china arms. *Private Collection.*

A Mystery China

There is still much to be learned about the history of dolls. Actually, no one is sure of the origin of this special china doll. However, since many of this type turn up in England, it is thought by some collectors that their origin is the Rockingham area of England. Others think they are French. Their date is probably 1840-1850. The quality of the china is excellent, with a natural complexion finish. The painted eyes are accented with an unpainted rectangle which provides a highlight; there is a black eyelash line and a red eyelid line. The color of the cheeks and mouth is quite vivid. The head has a closed dome covered by a wig; some heads have a molded slit for inserting the wig. The body is cloth with tinted china lower arms and legs. The lower limbs have holes for sewing them to the body instead of merely gluing them. This is the same method that the makers of English wax dolls use. If you are thinking of purchasing a doll of this type, be sure that it has the proper china lower limbs, which make the doll much more valuable than one on a full cloth body. No matter the origin, these are lovely quality dolls.

A China head lady with pink-tinted complexion and matching china lower arms and legs which tie on to a cloth body; human hair wig. This type of doll is also known in a child version with chubby face and limbs. *Richard Wright Antiques.*

COLLECTIBLE CHINA DOLLS

In 1939, Emma Clear advertised what she called "The First American China Doll." Mrs. Clear made reproductions of old chinas, including an 1840 head with bun (so-called *Mona Lisa*) and an 1870 head with bun (so-called *Jenny Lind*), a bonnet doll, a doll with molded hairbow (so-called *Dolley Madison*) and others. Mrs. Clear's dolls are excellent quality and well respected by collectors. To distinguish them from the originals, she marked them with a script "Clear" with the date inside the C. Some of her dolls were made from pink slip; some are bisque and not china.

Ruth Gibbs' dolls were made in Flemington, N.J., beginning

in 1946. They were pink or white china shoulder heads with china lower limbs on cotton bodies of plain or printed fabric. She called them *Godey's Little Lady Dolls* because they were in the old-fashioned style of the old china dolls and wore old-fashioned clothes, as well. Although of china, the dolls are not reproductions, but they are Miss Gibbs' interpretations of the old dolls. The Gibbs dolls have a simple 1860s molded and painted

Mrs. Clear had this original doll, *Danny Boy*, sculptured for her by Martha Oathout Ayers. Actually, *Danny* was a portrait of Martha Ayers' son. It was made in about 1914. Mrs. Ayers also sculptured Martha and George Washington dolls for Mrs. Clear. They apparently were very popular, so pairs are readily available on the secondary market. *Danny*, however, is seldom found. *H & J Foulke, Inc.*

blonde, red, black or brown hairstyle; the eyes have three long eyelashes at each side; mouths are heartshaped. Shoes are painted either gold or a color to match the hairstyle. The dolls are incised on the back shoulder plate "R G". The Gibbs dolls could be purchased dressed or undressed. *McCalls* published a pattern for making clothing for them. Popular with collectors now, Godey dolls in excellent original condition sell for $75 and up. Especially desirable is the March family of *Little Women*. Mrs. March is 12 inches (31 centimeter) and the girls are 7 inches (18 centimeter). Ruth Gibbs produced boxed gift and trousseau sets which are very sought after by avid Godey doll collectors.

TOP TO BOTTOM: A 7in (18cm) Ruth Gibbs doll in original old-fashioned cotton print outfit with typical felt Gibbs-style hat. Notice her distinctive face painting. She is made from glazed pink china and has gold shoes. The dolls had a rectangular paper label sewn inside the hem of the skirt giving the name and model number of the doll. *H & J Foulke, Inc.* A 12in (31cm) Ruth Gibbs lady doll with red hair and molded gold necklace and bracelet. The fancy gown is homemade. Some of the larger dolls had a more subdued eye treatment more like those of the old original chinas. *H & J Foulke, Inc.* 10in (25cm) *Godey's Little Lady Doll* with skin wig. She is from the 1951 *Good Fairy Queens* series and is #51-506 *Daisy Chain*. She is from pink china with gold slippers and large blue eyes. She is totally original. Wigged Gibbs dolls are very rare. *H & J Foulke, Inc.*

TIPS FOR COLLECTING CHINA HEAD DOLLS

1. As in any other area of collecting, always buy the best example that you can afford.

Quality. Look for an example with a smooth complexion and sharp modeling and with good painting detail in the face and hair. There may be a few black specks or pock marks, even some wear on the hair or a cheek rub. These are acceptable minor flaws so long as they don't interfere with your appreciation of the doll. Look for a doll with a face that appeals to you. Sometimes the special quality that makes a doll outstanding or the best example ever seen is very elusive and indefinable, but if you've looked at lots of dolls, you recognize the best when you see it.

Body. Look for a doll on an old cloth or cloth and leather body. Look for old china lower limbs. Try to find a doll with as much of the body old as possible. New cloth with old limbs is preferable to a totally new body. Keep in mind, however, that old cloth bodies are getting harder to find with every passing year. The older the cloth gets, the more apt it is to deteriorate.

Clothes. Look for an example with old clothes or at least appropriate new clothes. It is preferable for new clothes to be made from old fabrics in a style appropriate for the doll. Of course, original clothes would be the best possible find!

Condition. Look for a china head that has no cracks, chips or repairs. Small chips on the bottom of the shoulder plate are no problem. Check the shoulder plates carefully. It is sometimes hard for a beginner to see that a plate might have been repaired. The shoulder plate is a vulnerable spot for dolls. I wouldn't bother with a common doll that has been repaired, but a rare, early doll is another matter. As long as the price is right, I would consider buying a rare doll with a repaired plate. China limbs are another matter. I would rather have old repaired limbs than new limbs. I don't think repaired china limbs devalue the doll.

2. If you find a better example than one in your collection, you can always upgrade. Buy the better one and sell the lesser one. What would make a doll a better example? You might find one with a more appealing face, one with better painting, or one with much sharper modeling. You might find an example on a good old body with old limbs. This would be an upgrade from a doll on a new body. You might find an example with outstanding original clothes. This would be an upgrade from a doll with new clothes.

3. Shop around for the best doll at the best price. Since china head dolls are not the most popular dolls, sometimes you can get a good bargain. Always politely ask the dealer if there is a "better price." Remember, however, that you will have a better example if you buy one with an old body, limbs and clothes. You should expect to pay more for it than one with a new body and clothes.

4. Learn how to do minor repair work. Sometimes you can buy a good doll for less if the body needs some repair. Sometimes there are splits that can be patched. Be careful about buying dolls with splitting bodies, however, because they can easily get worse as they are handled. I've had them completely fall apart! Sometimes you can find a doll with a missing lower limb. It isn't impossible to find old replacement parts. You just have to look carefully for them wherever you go doll hunting.

5. Learn how to dress dolls appropriately. This doesn't necessarily mean that you need to sew the clothes yourself, although of course many collectors love this aspect of the hobby. But many dealers do sell old clothing and sometimes you can find clothes for a doll that you purchased for less because it was naked. If you do want to sew for your dolls, be sure to choose old fabrics and make the clothes in the appropriate style for the doll. Many china head dolls look wonderful in elaborate and fancy silk and satin gowns of the 1860s and 1870s. Some look better in simple cotton frocks with aprons and pinafores.

6. If you are buying at an auction, always inspect the doll before it comes up for sale. Never bid on a doll that you didn't examine. It may look great from your seat five rows back, but there may be pits and rubs on the face that you can't see from that distance. Also, if the doll is dressed, you can't tell whether or not the body and limbs are old and of the appropriate type for the doll. The doll may seem as if it is selling for a cheap price until you get it and see all of its problems!

7. Find other collectors with the same special interest as yours. Your best network for learning more about the type of doll you like most is other collectors and dealers. It is lots of fun to have someone with whom to share your finds and whose finds you can appreciate. If there is no one near you, look for someone at a regional or national convention. You can share photos of your dolls by mail. Discuss dolls with dealers at shows. They are always willing to share information about their dolls because they want you for a customer. However, don't take up a lot of a busy dealer's time if you have no intention of buying a doll. If you just want to talk about a doll or ask a question, pick a less busy time.

8. Last, but most important: enjoy your hobby!

ABOUT The Author, JAN FOULKE

The name Jan Foulke is synonymous with accurate information. As the author of the **Blue Book of Dolls & Values**®, heralded by *U.S.A. Today* as "The bible of doll collecting...", she is the most quoted source on doll information and the most respected and recognized authority on dolls and doll prices in the world.

Born in Burlington, New Jersey, Jan Foulke has always had a fondness for dolls. She recalls, "Many happy hours of my childhood were spent with dolls as companions, since we lived on a quiet county road, and until I was ten, I was an only child." Jan and her husband, Howard, who photographs the dolls presented in Jan's many titles, were both fond of antiquing as a hobby, and in 1972 they decided to open a small antique shop of their own. The interest of their daughter, Beth, in dolls sparked their curiosity about the history of old dolls – an interest that quite naturally grew out of their love of heirlooms. The stock in their antique shop gradually changed and evolved into an antique doll shop.

Early in the development of their antique doll shop, Jan and Howard realized that there was a critical need for an accurate and reliable doll identification and price guide resource. In the early 1970s, the Foulkes teamed up with Hobby House Press to produce (along with Thelma Bateman) the first **Blue Book of Dolls & Values,** originally published in 1974. Since that time, the Foulkes have exclusively authored and illustrated the eleven successive editions, which have sold over 1/2 million copies! Today the **Blue Book** is regarded by collectors and dealers as the definitive source for doll prices and values.

Jan and Howard Foulke now dedicate all of their professional time to the world of dolls: writing and illustrating books and articles, appraising collections, lecturing on antique dolls, acting as consultants to museums, auction houses and major collectors, and selling dolls both by mail order and through exhibits at major shows throughout the United States. Mrs. Foulke is a member of the United Federation of Dolls Clubs, Doll Collectors of America, and the International Doll Academy.

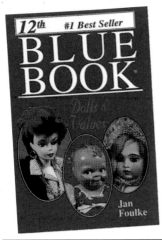

12th Blue Book Dolls & Values®

by Jan Foulke

You will find this classic identification and price guide book indispensable. The book features 516 photographs, 310 in color, of antique to collectible dolls. This is the guide that doll dealers use. With this book you are a doll appraiser! **#H4940 $17.95.**

"...the doll devotees bible"
The Washington Post

"The bible of doll collecting..."
U.S.A. Today

Save Money with any of these new books! Each book in the Insider's Guide Series to Doll Collecting is a treasure trove of tips on how to buy, sell, and collect dolls. Authored by Jan Foulke, a highly successful doll dealer, whose series of *Blue Books Dolls & Values* has sold over 1/2 million copies. Jan is the most quoted authority on dolls. Just one successful tip will get you back many times the cost of the book.

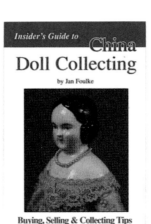

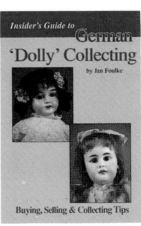

The Insider's Guide to
DOLL BUYING & SELLING:
Antique to Modern
by Jan Foulke
The beginner to the advanced collector or the antique to modern collector will find this book a must.
#H4944 $9.95

The Insider's Guide to
CHINA DOLL COLLECTING
by Jan Foulke
You will find a bonanza of buying, selling, and collecting tips for these antique dolls!
#H4943 $9.95

The Insider's Guide to
GERMAN 'DOLLY' COLLECTING
by Jan Foulke
Bisque girl doll lovers will find this book a treasure trove of buying, selling and collecting tips!
#H4945 $9.95